NFL ★ TEAM PROFILES

THE BALTIMORE RAVENS

BY THOMAS K. ADAMSON

EPIC

BELLWETHER MEDIA ★ MINNEAPOLIS, MN

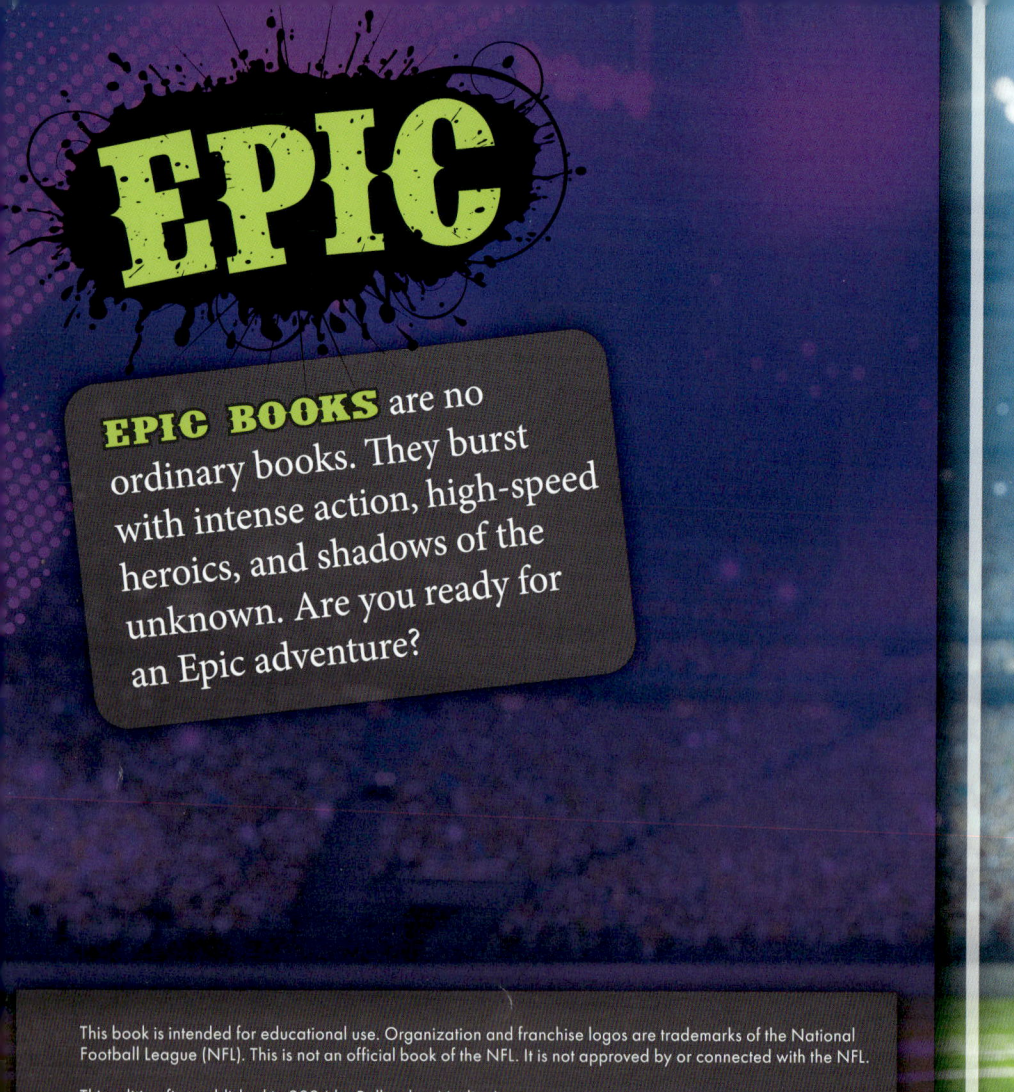

EPIC

EPIC BOOKS are no ordinary books. They burst with intense action, high-speed heroics, and shadows of the unknown. Are you ready for an Epic adventure?

This book is intended for educational use. Organization and franchise logos are trademarks of the National Football League (NFL). This is not an official book of the NFL. It is not approved by or connected with the NFL.

This edition first published in 2024 by Bellwether Media, Inc.

No part of this publication may be reproduced in whole or in part without written permission of the publisher. For information regarding permission, write to Bellwether Media, Inc., Attention: Permissions Department, 6012 Blue Circle Drive, Minnetonka, MN 55343.

Library of Congress Cataloging-in-Publication Data

Names: Adamson, Thomas K., 1970- author.
Title: The Baltimore Ravens / by Thomas K. Adamson.
Description: Minneapolis,MN : Bellwether Media, 2024. | Series: Epic. NFL team profiles | Includes bibliographical references and index. | Audience: Ages 7-12 | Audience: Grades 2-3 | Summary: "Engaging images accompany information about the Baltimore Ravens. The combination of high-interest subject matter and light text is intended for students in grades 2 through 7" Provided by publisher.
Identifiers: LCCN 2023021287 (print) | LCCN 2023021288 (ebook) | ISBN 9798886874686 (library binding) | ISBN 9798886876567 (ebook)
Subjects: LCSH: Baltimore Ravens (Football team)--History--Juvenile literature.
Classification: LCC GV956.B3 A43 2024 (print) | LCC GV956.B3 (ebook) | DDC 796.332/64097526--dc23/eng/20230517
LC record available at https://lccn.loc.gov/2023021287
LC ebook record available at https://lccn.loc.gov/2023021288

Text copyright © 2024 by Bellwether Media, Inc. EPIC and associated logos are trademarks and/or registered trademarks of Bellwether Media, Inc.

Editor: Elizabeth Neuenfeldt   Designer: Gabriel Hilger

Printed in the United States of America, North Mankato, MN.

TABLE OF CONTENTS

SUPER DEFENSE	4
THE HISTORY OF THE RAVENS	6
THE RAVENS TODAY	14
GAME DAY!	16
BALTIMORE RAVENS FACTS	20
GLOSSARY	22
TO LEARN MORE	23
INDEX	24

SUPER DEFENSE

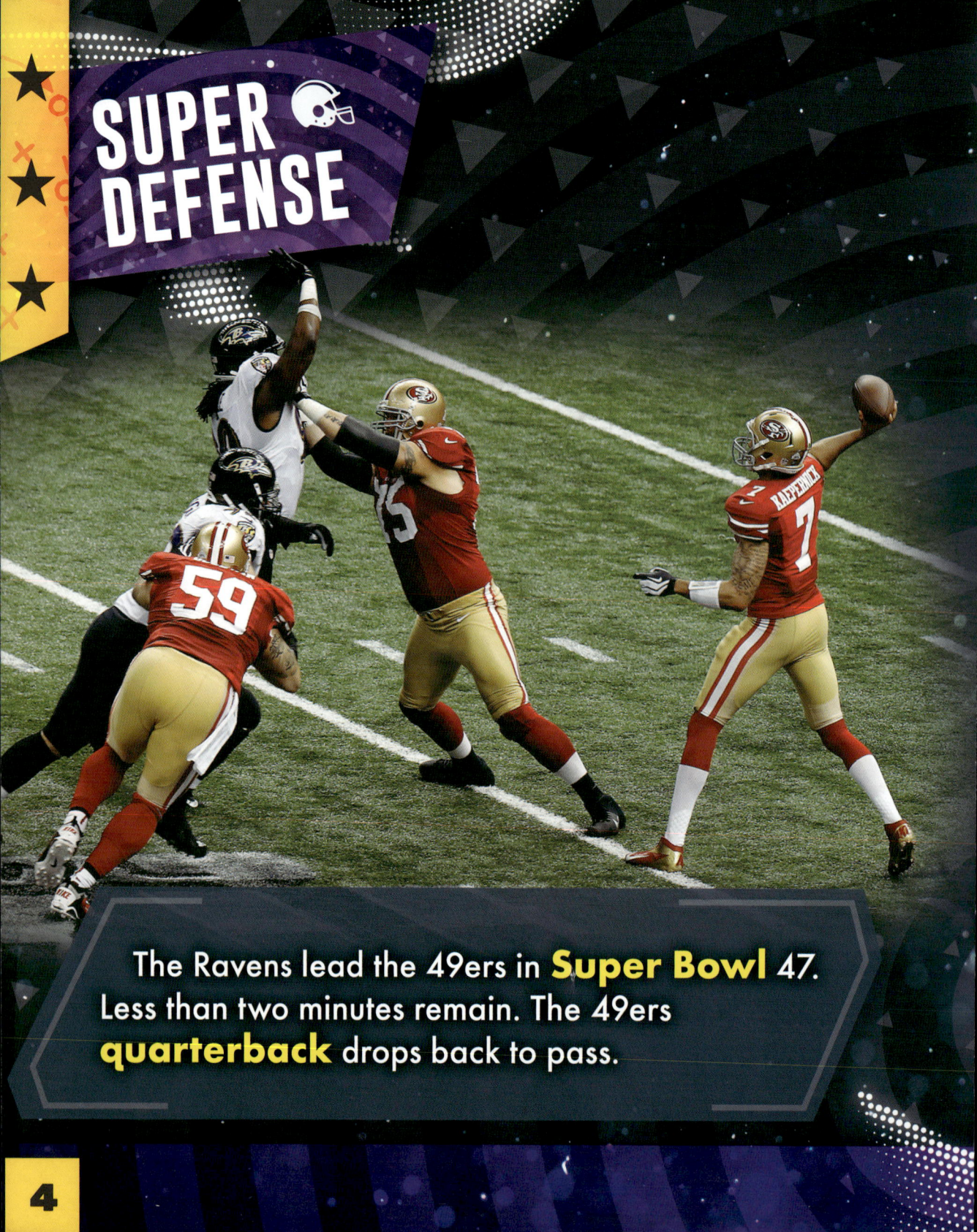

The Ravens lead the 49ers in **Super Bowl** 47. Less than two minutes remain. The 49ers **quarterback** drops back to pass.

The Ravens **defense** closes in. The pass is **incomplete**! The Ravens hold their lead. They win the Super Bowl!

THE HISTORY OF THE RAVENS

In 1996, the Cleveland Browns moved to Baltimore, Maryland. Team owners wanted a new name for the team's new city. The name Ravens honors the poet Edgar Allan Poe. He lived in Baltimore. He wrote a famous poem called "The Raven."

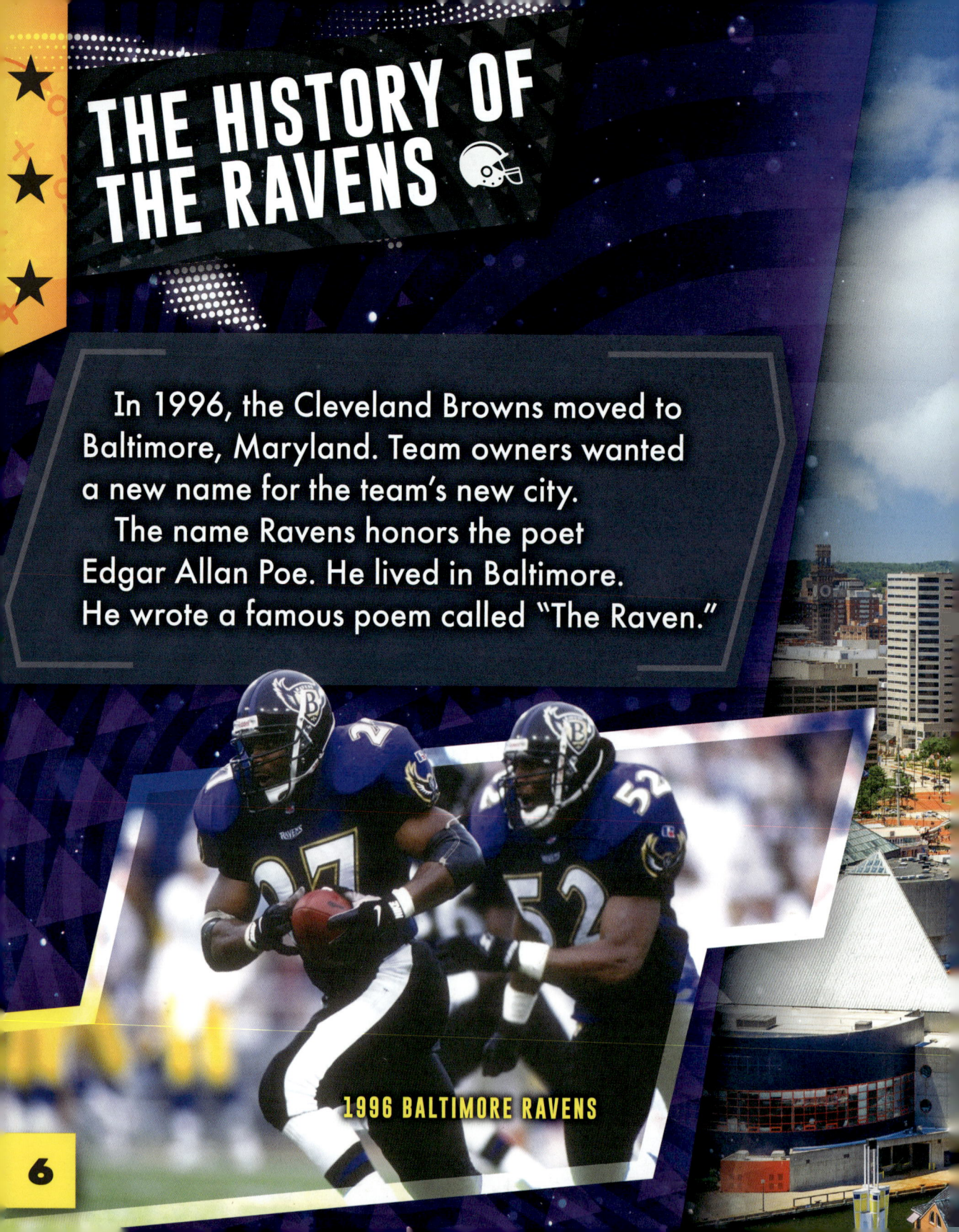

1996 BALTIMORE RAVENS

BALTIMORE, MARYLAND

THE BALTIMORE COLTS

Baltimore was once home to the Colts. They moved to Indianapolis, Indiana, in 1984. Baltimore was without a National Football League (NFL) team for 12 years.

7

The Ravens had success early on. They won Super Bowl 35 in 2001. It was only their fifth season!

SUPER BOWL 35

RAY LEWIS

Linebacker Ray Lewis was the **Most Valuable Player** (MVP) of Super Bowl 35. The Ravens became famous for their strong defense.

In 2008, the Ravens hired John Harbaugh. He is the team's longest serving head coach.

JOHN HARBAUGH

The Ravens kept playing well. In 2013, they won Super Bowl 47!

SUPER BOWL 47

In 2018, Lamar Jackson joined the team. In 2019, he broke the record for most **rushing** yards for a quarterback in one season. He became the NFL MVP!

🏆 TROPHY CASE 🏆

AFC NORTH championships
6

AFC championships
2

SUPER BOWL championships
2

13

THE RAVENS TODAY

RAVENS VS. STEELERS

The Ravens play their home games at M&T Bank **Stadium**. It is in Baltimore, Maryland.

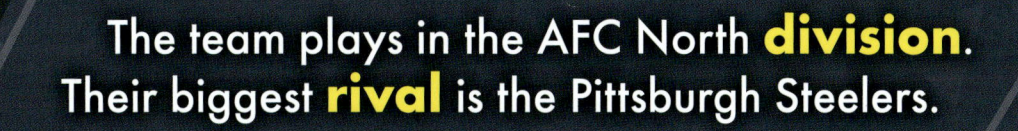

The team plays in the AFC North **division**. Their biggest **rival** is the Pittsburgh Steelers.

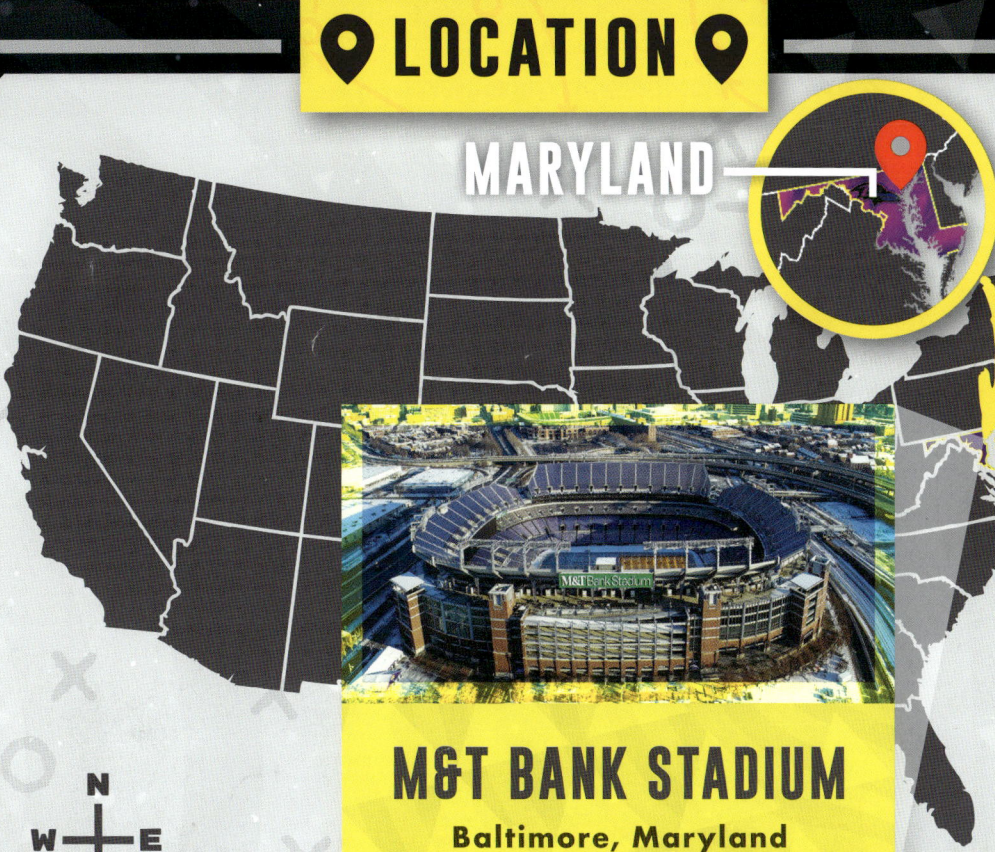

◉ LOCATION ◉

MARYLAND

M&T BANK STADIUM
Baltimore, Maryland

GAME DAY!

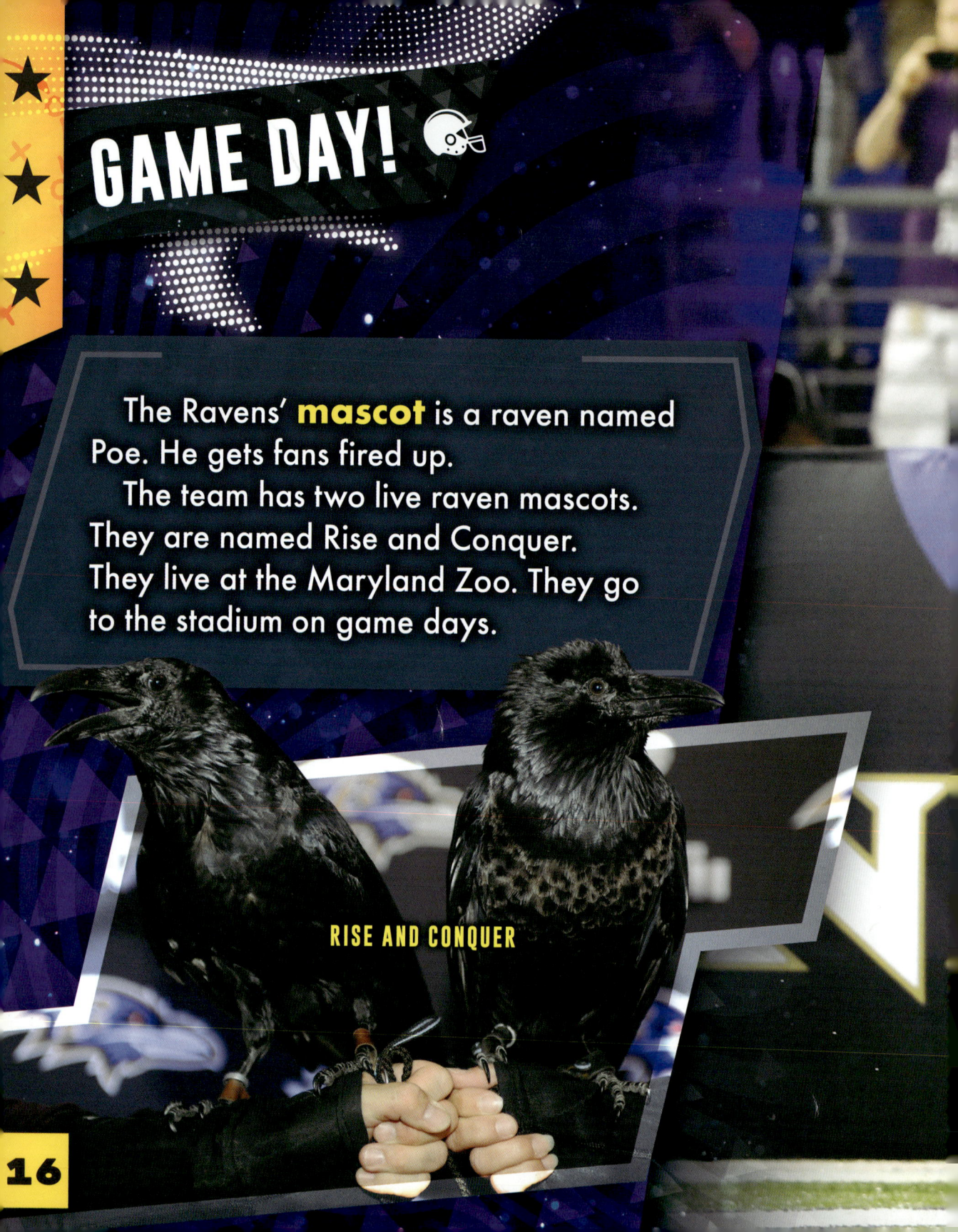

The Ravens' **mascot** is a raven named Poe. He gets fans fired up.

The team has two live raven mascots. They are named Rise and Conquer. They live at the Maryland Zoo. They go to the stadium on game days.

RISE AND CONQUER

Fans enjoy seeing the Marching Ravens at home games. It is the biggest music group in the NFL!

Fans sing the official Ravens fight song. It brings fans together when the Ravens score!

MARCHING RAVENS

MANY MARCHING RAVENS

More than 150 performers and crew members are a part of the Marching Ravens!

★ FAMOUS PLAYERS

52
RAY LEWIS
Linebacker
Played 1996–2012

31
JAMAL LEWIS
Running Back
Played 2000–2006

20
ED REED
Safety
Played 2002–2012

5
JOE FLACCO
Quarterback
Played 2008–2018

9
JUSTIN TUCKER
Kicker
Played 2012–present

BALTIMORE RAVENS FACTS

LOGO

| JOINED THE NFL | 1996 |

MASCOT

POE

| NICKNAME | Purple Pain |

CONFERENCE
American Football Conference (AFC)

COLORS

| DIVISION | AFC North |

 Cincinnati Bengals
 Cleveland Browns
 Pittsburgh Steelers

STADIUM

★ M&T BANK STADIUM ★
opened September 6, 1998

holds 71,008 people

20

⏱ TIMELINE

1996
The Cleveland Browns become the Baltimore Ravens

2001
The Ravens win Super Bowl 35

2008
John Harbaugh becomes the head coach of the Ravens

2013
The Ravens win Super Bowl 47

2020
Lamar Jackson wins the NFL MVP award

★ RECORDS ★

All-Time Passing Leader	All-Time Tackles Leader	All-Time Interceptions Leader	All-Time Scoring Leader

Joe Flacco
38,245 yards

Ray Lewis
1,568 tackles

Ed Reed
61 interceptions

Justin Tucker
1,502 points

21

GLOSSARY

defense—the group of players who try to stop the opposing team from scoring

division—a group of NFL teams from the same area that often play against each other; there are eight divisions in the NFL.

incomplete—not caught by anyone

linebacker—a player whose main job is to tackle opposing players

mascot—an animal or symbol that represents a sports team

Most Valuable Player—an award given to a player who contributes the most to their team's success

quarterback—a player whose main job is to throw and hand off the ball

rival—a long-standing opponent

rookie—a first-year player in a sports league

rushing—running with the ball

stadium—an arena where sports are played

Super Bowl—the annual championship game of the NFL

TO LEARN MORE

AT THE LIBRARY

Abdo, Kenny. *Baltimore Ravens*. Minneapolis, Minn.: Abdo Zoom, 2022.

Fishman, Jon M. *Lamar Jackson*. Minneapolis, Minn.: Lerner Publications, 2021.

Whiting, Jim. *The Story of the Baltimore Ravens*. Mankato, Minn.: Creative Education, 2020.

ON THE WEB

FACTSURFER

Factsurfer.com gives you a safe, fun way to find more information.

1. Go to www.factsurfer.com.

2. Enter "Baltimore Ravens" into the search box and click 🔍.

3. Select your book cover to see a list of related content.

INDEX

AFC North, 15, 20
Baltimore, Maryland, 6, 7, 14, 15
Baltimore Colts, 7
Baltimore Ravens facts, 20-21
Cleveland Browns, 6
colors, 20
defense, 5, 9
famous players, 19
fans, 16, 18
Flacco, Joe, 11
Harbaugh, John, 10
history, 4, 5, 6, 7, 8, 9, 10, 11, 12, 13
Jackson, Lamar, 13

Lewis, Ray, 9
Marching Ravens, 18
mascots, 16, 17, 20
Most Valuable Player, 9, 13
M&T Bank Stadium, 14, 15, 16, 20
name, 6
National Football League (NFL), 7, 13, 18, 20
Poe, Edgar Allan, 6
positions, 4, 9, 11, 13
records, 11, 13, 21
rival, 15
Super Bowl, 4, 5, 8, 9, 12
timeline, 21
trophy case, 13

The images in this book are reproduced through the courtesy of: Nick Wass/ AP Images, cover (hero); Paparacy, cover (stadium), p. 20 (stadium); UPI/ Alamy, p. 3; Kevin Terrell/ AP Images, p. 4; Al Bello/ Staff/ Getty, pp. 5, 6; Sean Pavone, pp. 6-7; Allen Kee/ Contributor/ Getty, p. 8; KMazur/ Contributor/ Getty, p. 9; Jim McIsaac/ Staff/ Getty, p. 10; Gregory Shamus/ Stringer/ Getty, pp. 10-11; Lexington Herald-Leader/ Contributor/ Getty, p. 12; Patrick Smith/ Staff/ Getty, pp. 14, 21 (Justin Tucker), 23; Nicole Glass Photography, p. 15 (M&T Bank Stadium); NFL/ Wikipedia, pp. 15 (Baltimore Ravens logo), 19 (Baltimore Ravens logo, Cincinnati Bengals logo, Cleveland Browns logo, Pittsburgh Steelers logo, AFC logo); Larry French/ AP Images, pp. 16, 18-19; Rob Carr/ Staff/ Getty, pp. 16-17, 21 (Joe Flacco); Focus On Sport/ Contributor/ Getty, pp. 19 (Ray Lewis), 21 (Ray Lewis); Greg Fiume/ Stringer/ Getty, p. 19 (Jamal Lewis); Icon Sportswire/ Contributor/ Getty, p. 19 (Ed Reed); Jeff Gross/ Staff/ Getty, p. 19 (Joe Flacco); Tribune Content Agency LLC/ Alamy, p. 19 (Justin Tucker); Julio Cortez/ AP Images, p. 20 (mascot); George Gojkovich/ Contributor/ Getty, p. 21 (1996); DOUG MONACO/ Contributor/ Getty, p. 21 (2001); Rob Tringali/ Sportschrome/ Contributor/ Getty, p. 21 (2008); Jamie Squire/ Staff/ Getty, p. 21 (2013); Patrick Semansky/ AP Images, p. 21 (2020); ZUMA Press Inc/ Alamy, p. 21 (Ed Reed).